DISCOVER

Stars

by Libby Romero

Table of Contents

Introduction

Stars are **gas**. Stars are in the **universe**.

▲ The universe has stars.

Words to Know

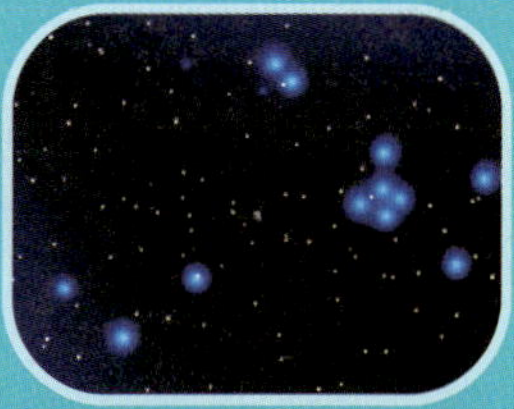

constellations

disappear

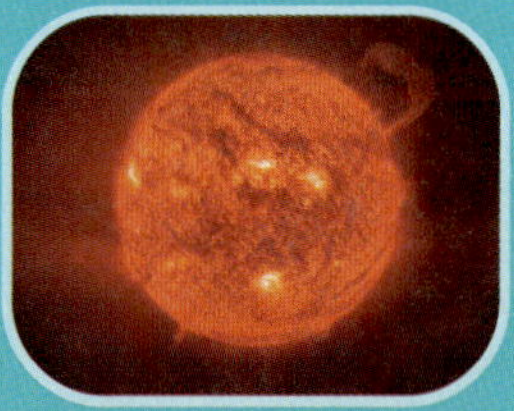

gas

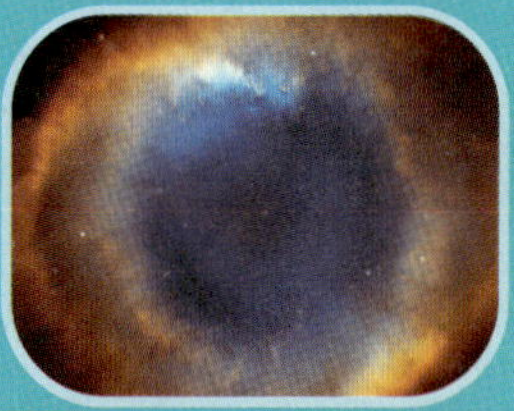

nebulas

stars

universe

See the Glossary on page 22.

What Are Stars?

Stars are living.

▲ These stars are living.

It's a Fact

The sun is a star.

Stars are balls of burning gas.

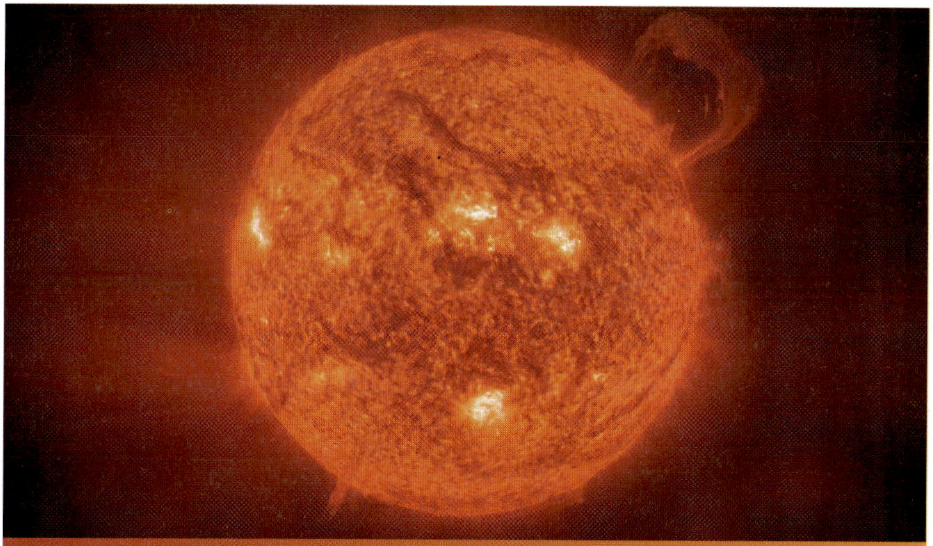

▲ This star is gas.

Stars are different colors.

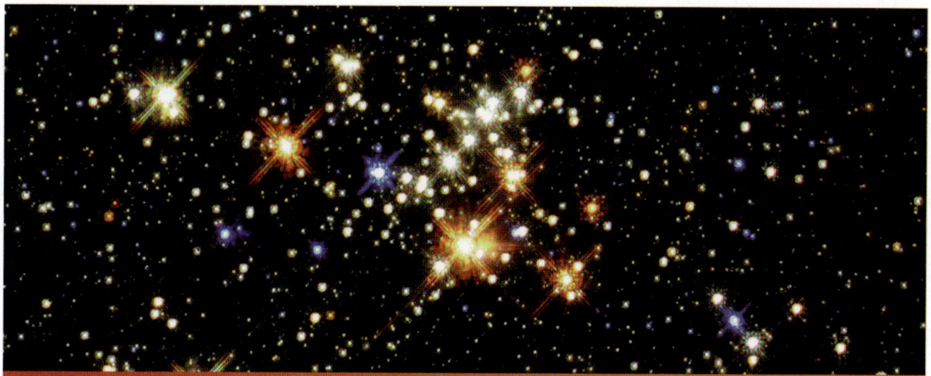

▲ These stars are different colors.

Some stars are huge.

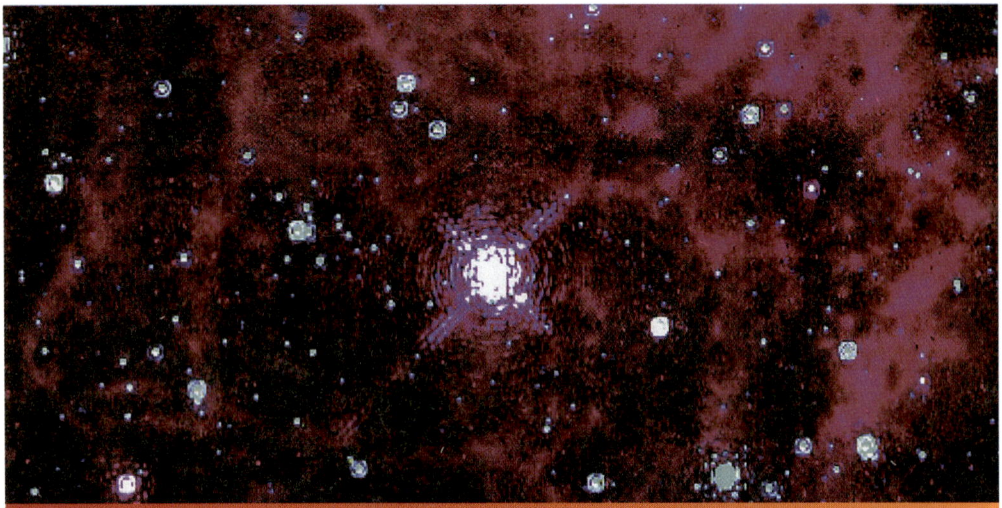

▲ This star is huge.

Some stars are small.

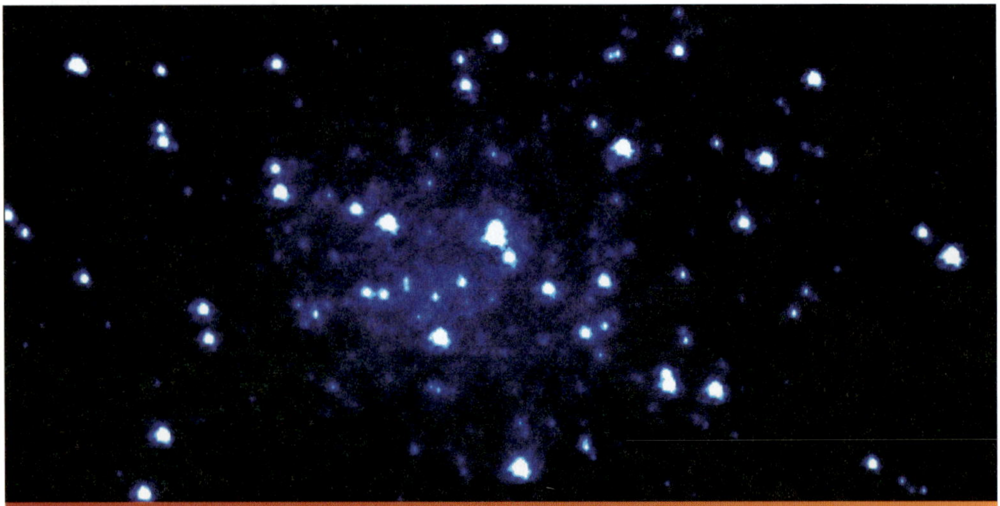

▲ These stars are small.

Some stars are in groups. Some stars are in **constellations**.

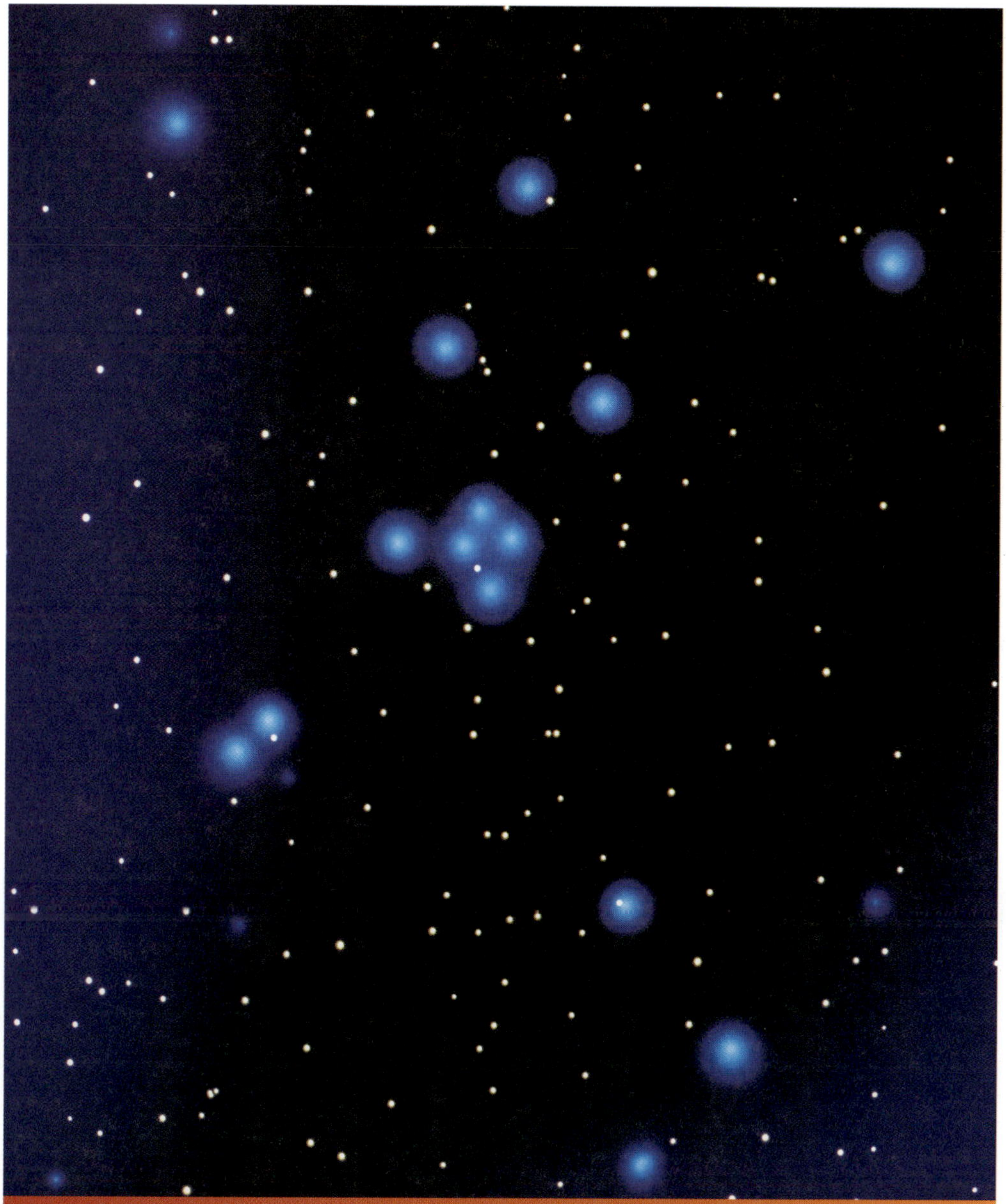

▲ **These stars are in a constellation.**

What Happens to Stars?

Stars begin in **nebulas**.

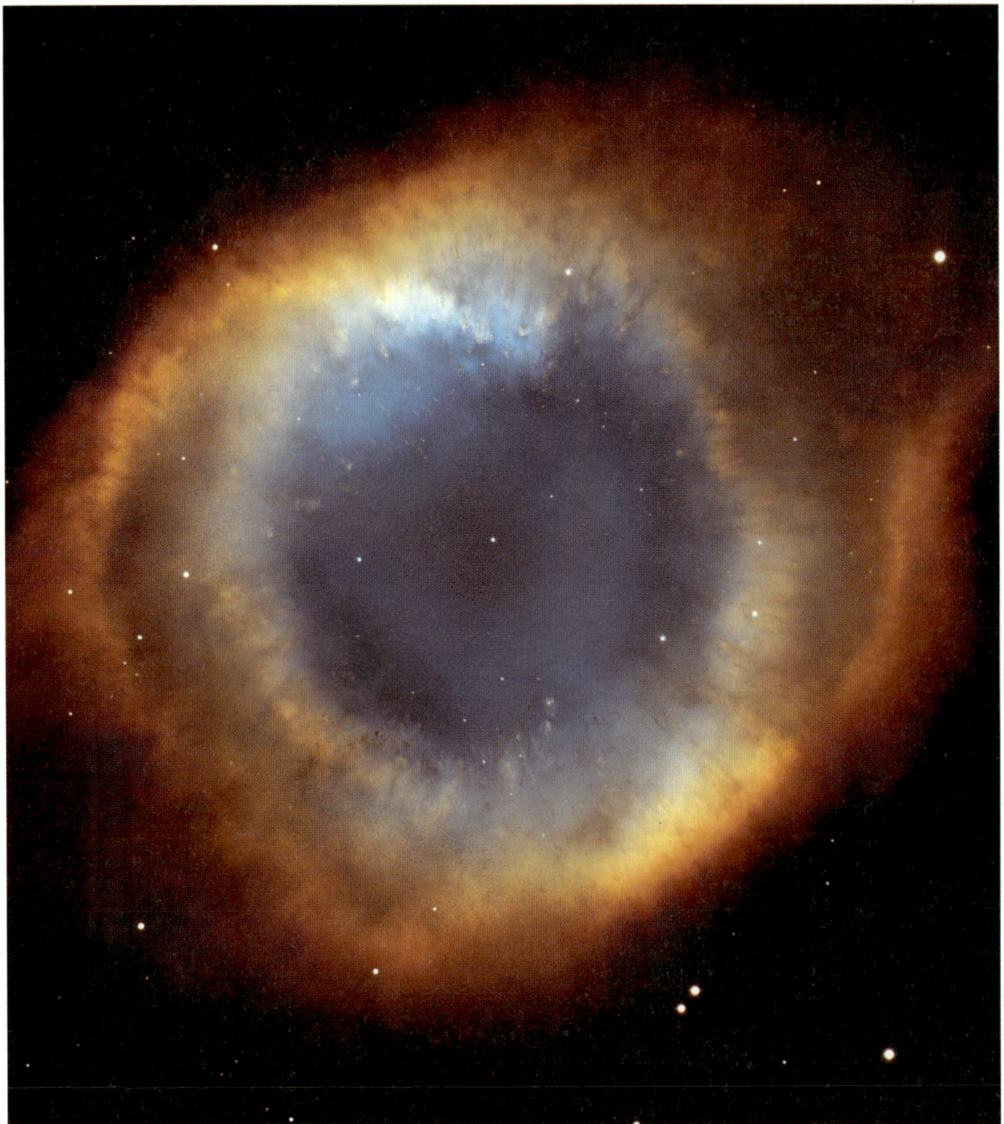

▲ **This star begins in a nebula.**

Stars begin to grow.

▲ This star begins to grow.

Stars begin to live.

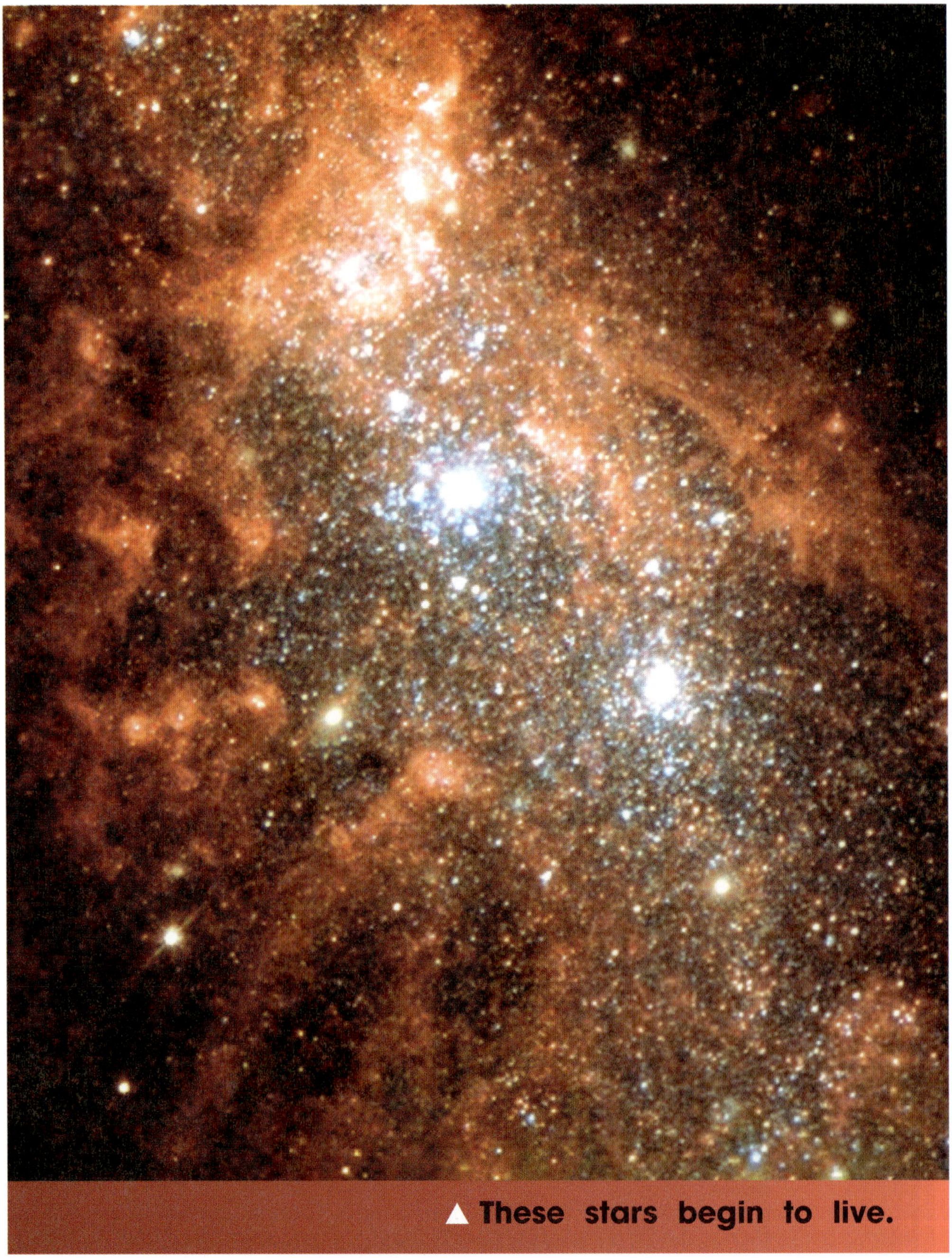

▲ These stars begin to live.

Stars begin to die.

▲ This star begins to die.

It's a Fact

Some stars explode.

▲ This star explodes.

Stars begin to lose light.

▲ This star begins to lose light.

Some stars begin to **disappear**.

▲ **This star begins to disappear.**

Who Studies Stars?

People study stars.

▲ **People watch stars.**

It's a Fact

People made maps of the stars. The maps helped people find places.

Students study stars.

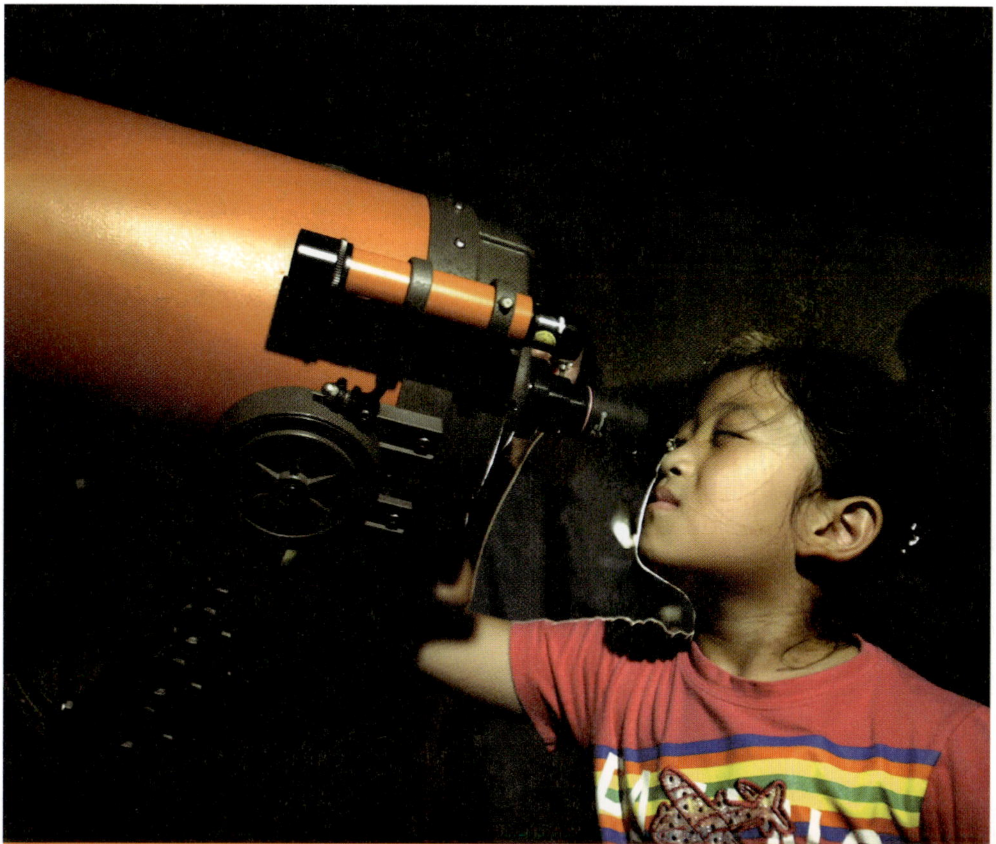

▲ **Students watch stars.**

Astronomers study stars.

▲ Astronomers watch stars.

Scientists study stars.

▲ Scientists watch stars.

Conclusion

Stars are balls of burning gas. Stars are in the universe. Stars are important to people.

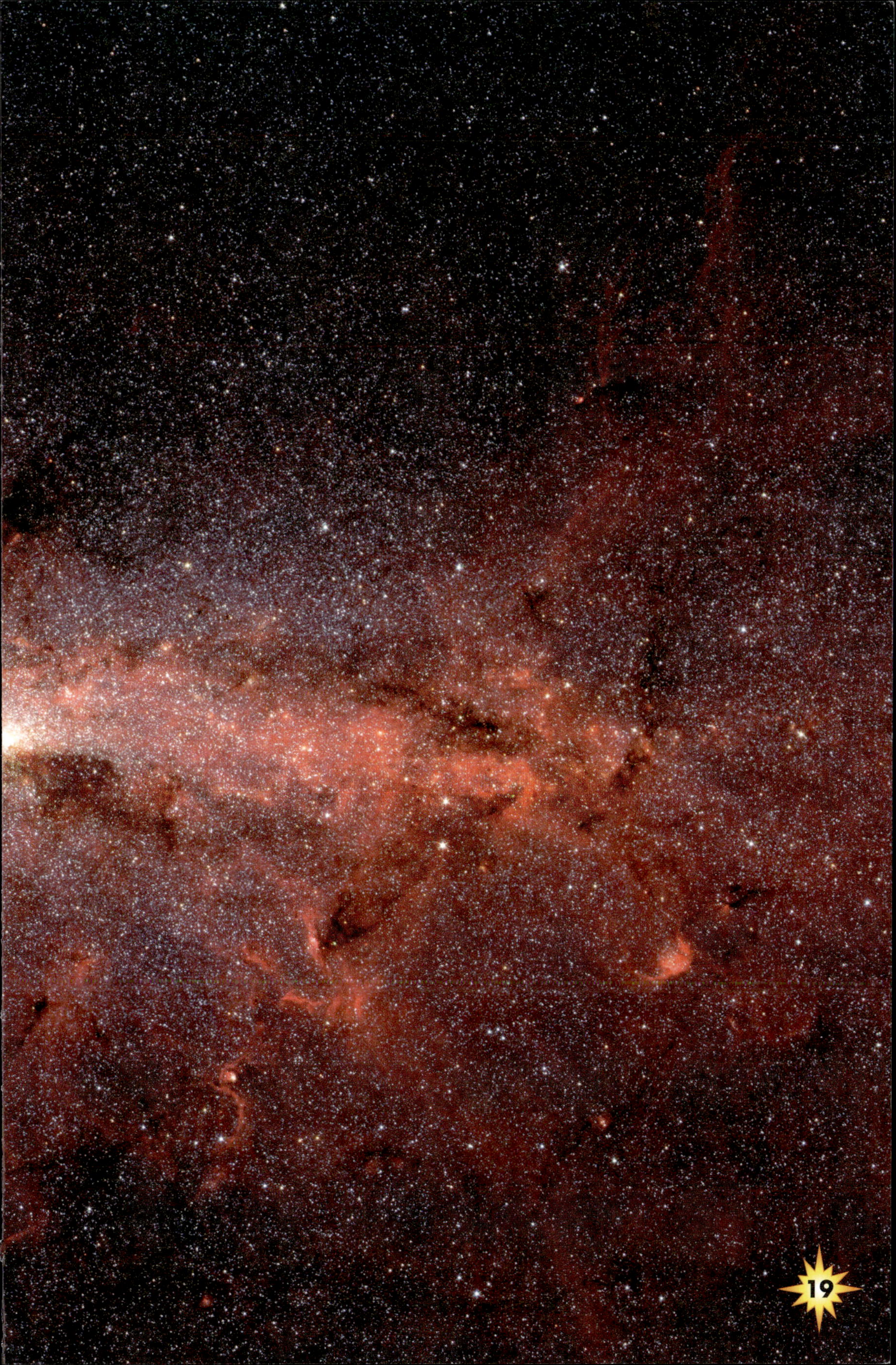

Concept Map

Stars

What Are Stars?	What Happens to Stars?
living	begin in nebulas
balls of burning gas	begin to grow
different colors	begin to live
huge	begin to die
small	begin to lose light
some in constellations	begin to disappear

Who Studies Stars?

- people
- students
- astronomers
- scientists

Glossary

constellations groups of stars

*Some stars are in **constellations**.*

disappear to go away

*Some stars begin to **disappear**.*

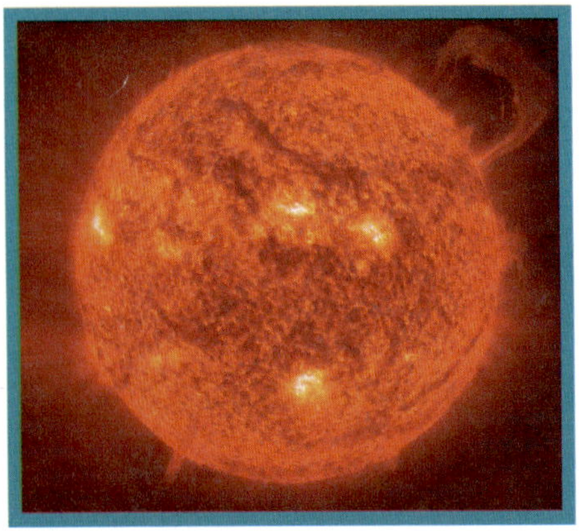

gas matter with no shape

*Stars are balls of burning **gas**.*

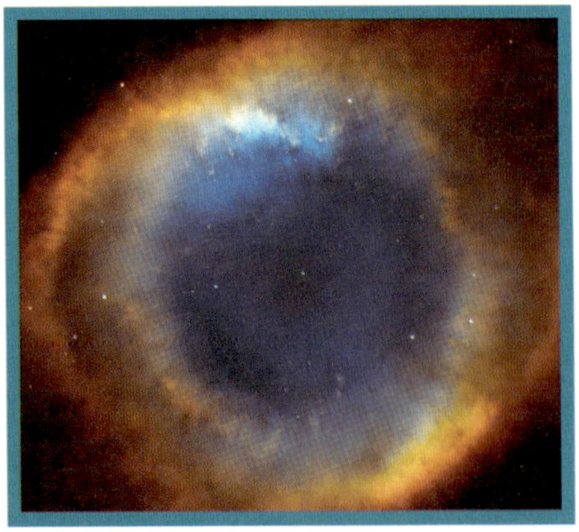

nebulas giant dust and gas clouds in space

*Stars begin in **nebulas**.*

stars huge balls of gas

Stars *are living.*

universe everything in space

Stars are in the ***universe****.*

Index